Ultimate Cars

LAMBORGHINI

A.T. McKenna

ABDO Publishing Company

visit us at
www.abdopub.com

Published by Abdo Publishing Company, 4940 Viking Drive, Edina, Minnesota 55435.
Copyright © 2000 by Abdo Consulting Group, Inc. International copyrights reserved in all
countries. No part of this book may be reproduced in any form without written permission from
the publisher.

Printed in the United States.

Cover and Interior Photo credits: Automobili Lamborghini, Corbis, and David Gooley

Library of Congress Cataloging-in-Publication Data

McKenna, A. T.
    Lamborghini / A. T. McKenna.
        p.   cm. -- (Ultimate cars)
    Includes index.
    Summary: Surveys the history of the Lamborghini and its designs, engines, and performance.
     ISBN 1-57765-125-1
    1. Lamborghini automobile -- Juvenile literature. [1. Lamborghini automobile.]
  I. Title. II. Series.
    TL2155.L33M377 2000
    629.222'1--dc21

                                      98-6647
                                         CIP
                                         AC

Revised Edition 2002

Contents

Italy's Other Sports Car

Legend has it that Ferruccio Lamborghini was so disappointed with his Ferrari, that he decided to build his own sports car. A sports car is a fast car with a sporty look. It is designed for the fun of driving. Sports cars most often have only two seats.

Some of the most famous sports car manufacturers come from Italy. They include Lamborghini, Ferrari, Maserati, Fiat, and Alfa Romeo.

The Lamborghini Diablo

The Lamborghini factory is located in St. Agata, Italy, about 15 miles (24 km) from Bologna and Modena. Lamborghinis, like Ferraris, are produced in small series for a few wealthy customers. The factory never made more than 500 cars per year.

The Espada is the most common Lamborghini model, with a total of 1,217 units made. Other Lamborghini models include the Diablo, Countach, Miura, Portofino, Cheetah, Jalpa, and Genesis.

Lamborghini's logo is a strong, charging bull. Lamborghini used the symbol to distinguish his cars from Ferraris, which have a prancing horse logo. Most of Lamborghini's car models are named after famous fighting bulls or breeds of fighting bulls.

**Lamborghini's
official logo**

Ferruccio Lamborghini

Ferruccio Lamborghini was born on April 28, 1916, in Renazzim, Italy. It is a small village near Bologna, Italy. Renazzim was in the Po Valley, an area famous for its automobile industry.

Ferruccio's family farmed the land. But, Ferruccio was better at fixing farm equipment than actually farming. So, his family sent him to a technical school to become a mechanic.

After graduating, Ferruccio was drafted into the army. He was stationed on the island of Rhodes in the Mediterranean Sea. Because of his mechanical ability, Ferruccio was placed in charge of army trucks and command cars. He was a mechanical genius. Ferruccio was able to fix equipment even when the proper parts were not available. He just found other parts that would work instead.

When the war ended, Ferruccio returned to the family farm. He found that there was a shortage of farm tractors. So, he started to make homemade tractors. Soon, the Lamborghini Tractor Company was one of the largest in Italy.

After the success of his tractor company, Ferruccio started a new business. It made heating and cooling equipment, such as oil burners and air conditioners. This business was very successful as well. Ferruccio was now one of the richest men in Italy.

Ferruccio Lamborghini

Ferruccio's Fast Car

Ever since Ferruccio was a boy, he had dreamed of starting his own car company. He liked fast cars and even competed in some races. Ferruccio's biggest race was the 1948 Mille Miglia. He ended the race by accidently driving through the room of a small roadside hotel. After that experience, Ferruccio decided he would only drive fast cars on the freeway, or *autostrada* as it is called in Italy.

Ferruccio owned a Ferrari. It was one of the fastest cars in Italy at the time. Yet this speedy car gave off smoke and a burning smell when Ferruccio drove it fast. He was not happy with this car, and decided to go to the Ferrari headquarters and tell owner Enzo Ferrari just that.

The two men disagreed on the cause of the smoke problem. Ferruccio vowed to create a car better than a Ferrari. So in 1962, Ferruccio began building the first Lamborghini. He was able to hire the best car builders, many of whom used to work for Ferrari.

First Ferruccio needed an engine builder. Ferruccio found former Ferrari engine builder Giotto Bizzarrini. He was an expert at building high-performance engines. At the time, Bizzarrini had been working on a V-12 engine. He promised Ferruccio that he would build an engine bigger than any Ferrari engine.

Bizzarrini created a 3.5 liter V-12, which produced 360 horsepower at 8,000 rpm. The number after *V* stands for how many cylinders the engine has. Horsepower is the amount of power the engine has. The initials *rpm* stand for revolutions per minute. This means that while the engine is running, it goes through the same sequence of events thousands of times per minute to keep the fuel flowing through the engine.

Next the car needed a chassis. The chassis is the frame of the car. It looks like the car's skeleton. Two young engineers named Giampaolo Dallara and Paolo Stanzani worked together to create the first Lamborghini chassis. It had a frame made of steel tubes. The body was made of thin aluminum plating to save weight.

While the engine and chassis for the first car where produced at Lamborghini, the design and construction of the car's body was done elsewhere. Traditionally, the bodies of Italian cars were built by *carrozzerias*, which means "coach (car) builders" in Italian. The car's body is made up of the panels which fit over the chassis. The body is usually handcrafted. Lamborghini chose Carrozzeria Touring to design and build the body for his first car and many of his other cars. This first car was called the 350GT. The letters *GT* stand for "Grand Touring."

Opposite page: The Lamborghini 350 GT. From 1964-1966, Lamborghini built 120 350GTs.

Famous Lamborghini People

There are many people at Lamborghini who helped build Italy's famous sports car. The founder of Lamborghini is, of course, Ferruccio Lamborghini. He started the car building company in 1962 and sold the company in 1973. After he retired, Ferruccio moved to Perugia and began making wine from his vineyards. He died in 1993.

In 1962, Giampaolo Dallara joined Lamborghini as chief engineer. He is considered one of the best chassis engineers of all time. Before working at Lamborghini, he had worked at Ferrari and Maserati. Dallara was responsible for engineering the Miura. He worked on the Miura with Bob Wallace and Paolo Stanzani.

Paolo Stanzani succeeded Dallara as chief engineer in 1968. Stanzani used to work for Maserati. At Lamborghini, he worked on the Miura, helping to rid it of flaws. But he is most remembered for engineering the legendary Countach.

Marcello Gandini is one of the world's greatest car designers. He worked for Abarth and Bertone, where he was responsible for many Lamborghini designs, including the

Miura, Espada, Jarama, Urraco, and Countach.

Giotto Bizzarrini was an engineer for Ferrari and Alfa Romeo. He came to Lamborghini in 1962 to built Lamborghini's V-12 engine. His engine was called the 350GTV.

Bob Wallace had worked as a racing

Bizzarrini's 12-cylinder engine was used in all Lamborghini cars, including the Countach.

mechanic for Maserati and Ferrari. Wallace started to work for Lamborghini as a test driver. He tested the different models by driving them and giving a report on their performance. He soon became the head of the testing department.

Luigi Marmiroli was the technical director responsible for the Diablo. He used to work for Alfa Romeo.

Giulio Alfieri was Lamborghini's technical director. He oversaw the development of the Countach and the Jalpa.

Creating a Car

Ferruccio knew more than anyone that building a car isn't an easy task. He was fortunate to have designers and engineers who had lots of experience. Most had worked for Ferrari, Maserati, or Alfa Romeo before joining Lamborghini.

In order to build a car, it takes hundreds of people, from designers and engineers to mechanics to assembly line crews. First, the design department comes up with an idea of how the car should look. Then, the designer usually draws several versions of the car before it is accepted.

Next, designers use wood and foam to make a frame. This frame is the actual size of the car. Warm clay is laid on the frame to make a life-sized model of the car.

Today, computers are often used to design cars. Automobile designers use Computer Aided Design (CAD) techniques. Once the basic shape of the car is decided, the clay model of the car is scanned onto the computer. The designer can then change the design with the touch of a button.

The design of the car must be approved by the executives of the company. Once it is approved, engineers work with mechanics to build a prototype.

A prototype is a very early version of the car. All the parts on the prototype are tested for strength and quality. Bob Wallace of Lamborghini test drove the prototypes on the streets of Italy and at race tracks nearby. The prototype is also displayed at car shows to get people's responses before the actual cars are produced.

A prototype of the Lamborghini Diablo

After much research is done on the prototype, executives at the company decide whether or not to build the car. If the car is going to be built, changes are made based on the results of the testing and the responses of the people who saw it.

Next, it is time to build the car for the public. Most cars go through an assembly line when being built. An assembly line is a system used to produce many kinds of products, such as cars.

Each worker has a specific job to do. The workers line up in rows and perform their jobs as the car moves down the line. One worker may put in the steering wheel, while another installs the engine. The assembly line was not what we think of today, with machinery doing a lot of the work. The Lamborghini assembly line was more of a production line. One car was produced at a time and the engine was assembled separately then placed in the chassis.

**Workers on an assembly line in St. Agata,
Italy, build a Lamborghini.**

Lamborghini Timeline

350 GT

The Miura

The Espada

The Countach

The Diablo

The Miura

Lamborghini's Miura was first presented at the 1966 Geneva Motor Show. Its steel chassis had been shown a year earlier at the Turin Motor Show.

Miura production began in 1967. It was so popular that the factory had a hard time keeping up with the demand. The Miura became the first Lamborghini to gain widespread recognition. It was the car that made Lamborghini famous.

A *carrozzeria* called Bertone designed the Miura's body. The Bertone designer was Marcello Gandini. He was young and came up with some fresh ideas for the car. The body was not flashy, but sleek and classic looking. The headlights had little vertical lines above and below them, which looked like eyelashes.

The V-12 engine was mounted in the middle of the car. Since the engine did not take up any room in the front, the Miura's hood was flat and low. Top speed for the Miura was 171 mph (275 km/h).

The Miura was built from 1967 until 1972. About 763 cars were built total.

***The Miura is named after the famous Spanish
bull breeder, Don Eduardo Miura.***

The Espada

The Espada was introduced at the Geneva Motor Show in 1968. It had a V-12 engine mounted in the front. The Espada's top speed was around 155 mph (250 km/h) at 7500 rpm.

The chassis was made of a steel platform, not tubes like in earlier cars. The Espada was wide and bulky, but it looked slim from many angles. At 186.5 inches (474 cm), the Espada was the same length as many of the compact cars in the United States during the late 1960s.

The Espada was the first Lamborghini to have four seats instead of two. It was the fastest four-seater on the market. Demand was great for this fast, stylish "family car." Owners could fit more people in the car than ever before, even though space was still a bit tight.

The Espada was a very popular car. Many were exported to the United States. The U.S. had strict safety laws. So, the Espadas exported to the U.S. had to have special heavy black bumpers on them for safety reasons.

Espada production ended in 1978. There were 1,217 Espadas made during the car's 10-year history. It was the most successful Lamborghini yet.

The word espada **is Spanish for the
sword bullfighters use.**

The Countach

The last car Ferruccio helped design was the Countach. Paolo Stanzani was chief designer and engineer of the Countach. His assistant, Massimo Parenti, had helped with the Miura.

The first Countach came off the assembly line in 1972. It had lots of slits cut into the body to let air flow through, which made it look like a fighter jet. Its first production year was 1973. That year, only 23 Countachs were delivered.

Engine builder Giulio Alfieri joined Lamborghini to help rework the V-12 engine. The Countach's engine was still placed in the middle of the car. The top speed for the Countach was 171 mph (275 km/h). But test-driver Bob Wallace clocked 180.2 mph (290 km/h) at 7600 rpm in the very first Countach.

A new feature on the Countach was the method of opening the doors. A hidden button inside the air ducts on the side of the car released the doors. They swung up easily on single hinges. The doors opened up vertically, sticking straight up in the air.

In 1990, the last Countach rolled off the assembly line. Five different Countach models were made and 1,972 total cars were produced in the Countach's 18-year lifetime.

The word countach is an Italian slang word that means "wow, unbelievable!"

The Diablo

After the Countach came the Diablo, designed by Marcello Gandini. The Diablo debuted at Monte Carlo in 1990. This was the first Lamborghini car to reach 200 mph (322 km/h). This was also the first Lamborghini to be used in Formula One racing.

The Diablo's chassis was made of welded steel tubes, which were square instead of round like those in the Countach. Most of the body was made of aluminum alloy, but the floor panels, trunk, and hood were made of carbon fiber. Carbon fiber is several woven pieces of a material that are very strong. It is dark in color and looks like fiberglass.

At 175.5 inches long (446 cm) and 80.3 inches wide (204 cm), the Diablo was a large car. And, it was heavy, weighing 3,640 pounds (1,651 kg).

The Diablo has the famous front-hinged, swing-up doors. When a driver wants to open the door, he or she pushes a button and the door releases, standing straight up in the air!

In 1991, Lamborghini offered a four-wheel drive Diablo VT. Four-wheel drive means the power from the engine is sent to all four wheels of the car. In regular cars, the engine power is just sent to two of the four wheels, either the front or the rear. The *VT* stands for viscous traction.

The Diablo SE30 was a special edition model limited to 30 cars. It marked the thirtieth anniversary of the first Lamborghini car. It could reach a speed of 206 mph (331 km/h) at 7,100 rpm. Each of the 30 cars had a numbered plate below the left window, telling the order in which the particular car was produced. With only 30 SE30s on the road, this car is very rare.

The Diablo was named after a famous Spanish fighting bull.

Ferruccio Retires

In 1973 Ferruccio sold 51 percent of his company to Henri Rossetti of Switzerland. He gave up active management of the company. Then, in 1974, he sold the other 49 percent of the company to Rene Daimer, a friend of Rossetti.

Ferruccio said he sold the company because he feared the new, slower speed limits would hurt his business. Speed limits had been reduced to 87 mph (140 km/h), and Ferruccio though drivers wouldn't have a need for his fast cars. Ferruccio also worried that the high cost of gasoline would make the cars too expensive to run. And, there was talk of prohibiting driving on Saturdays and Sundays. These are the two days most sports car owners a take their cars for a drive.

The company faced a few years of uncertainty until Patrick Mimran bought the company in 1981. He owned Lamborghini until 1987, when Chrysler Corporation took over.

Chrysler lost interest in Lamborghini in the early 1990s because it was losing money. The factory was closed for more than three months in 1992. Chrysler then put Lamborghini up for sale. In 1993, the company was bought by MegaTech, an Indonesian company.

During the 1990s, Lamborghini continued to create new and exciting designs, such as the Jotto.

Glossary

carrozzeria - companies that built the bodies of the cars for Lamborghini.

Computer Aided Design (CAD) - computer software that allows a person to design a car by using a computer.

debut - the first public appearance.

cylinder - the chamber in the engine where fuel is burned.

debut - the first public appearance.

drafted - to be selected for military service. People who are drafted must serve in the armed forces.

duct - a tube, pipe, or channel that carries something, such as a liquid or a gas.

executive - a person who directs or manages a company's affairs.

fiberglass - a durable, nonflammable material that is made from fine threads of glass.

Formula One - a kind of race in which people drive single-seat cars. The insides of the cars have no luxuries, only the basic instruments required for driving.

import - to bring an object, such as a car, from one country into another country for sale or trade.

plating - a thin coating or layer or metal, such as silver or gold.

performance - the way in which a car handles.

scan - to pass an electric beam over an image. The beam converts the image to electronic properties, which allows the scanned image to be altered or transferred by a computer.

series - Lamborghinis that are similar to one another are grouped into what is called a series. A series usually lasts several years. All the cars in the series usually have a similar body shape and style.

technical school - a school in which students are trained in a specific profession, such as science or art.

viscous traction - a system that automatically switches the power between front and rear differentials to prevent slipping. Differentials are the gears that allow the opposite driving wheels of a car to turn at different speeds when the vehicle rounds a curve.

Internet Sites

Automobili Lamborghini Web Site
http://www.lamborghini.com

Lamborghini's official web site has a history of the company, lots of Lamborghini photographs, and model specifications. This site also has information about Lamborghini race cars.

These sites are subject to change. Go to your favorite search engine and type in "Lamborghini" for more sites.

Index